GANGSTERS

—— PORTRAITS IN CRIME ——

JOSHUA B. FEDER

Friedman Group

DEDICATION

To my students, past and present, for all they have taught me.

ACKNOWLEDGMENTS

I would like to thank the staff of the New York Public Library for their patient assistance during my long hours of research.

A FRIEDMAN GROUP BOOK

Copyright © 1992 by Michael Friedman Publishing Group, Inc.

ISBN 0 7924 5691 2

GANGSTERS
was prepared and produced by
Michael Friedman Publishing Group, Inc.
15 West 26th Street
New York, New York   10010

Editor: Nathaniel Marunas
Art Director: Jeff Batzli
Designer: Lynne Yeamans
Photography Editor: Daniella Jo Nilva

Colour separation by Bright Arts Pte. Ltd.
Printed and bound in Hong Kong by
Leefung-Asco Printers Ltd.

C O N T E N T S

INTRODUCTION

You may assume that crime, too, is incorporated.

          —Thomas Dewey, 1937

Citizens of the United States, Canada, Australia, and Great Britain, despite what they might say about each other, have much in common. Not only is English the first language, but day-to-day life in these industrialized, urbanized, and wealthy nations is governed by remarkably similar legal and political traditions. The roughly 350 million citizens of these four nations have something else in common: they share the dubious honor of being exploited by some of the most highly organized criminal organizations in the entire world.

Organized crime is run by gangsters, but gangsters are no ordinary criminals. They are not

Rum runners made fortunes during the Prohibition era. Spectators look on as New York officials unload 3,900 cases of liquor seized from a Canadian ship in January 1931.

Al Capone was one of the most flamboyant and well-known gangsters of all time. At the height of his reign in Chicago, he maintained a full gymnasium for his army of thugs.

petty thieves or sporadic felons. By definition, a gangster is part of an organized group of individuals devoted to breaking the law on a systematic and continual basis. Gangsters run rackets, illegal scams that are made possible by bribery or intimidation. The profits generated from these rackets inevitably flow upward, toward the high-level bosses who mastermind these operations.

Whether you are talking about the Mafia (which is of Italian origin), the South American drug cartels, the Japanese *yakuza* ("good for nothings"), or the Chinese triads,

the bottom line is that crime is their business. Gangsters, for all intents and purposes, conduct business like any other corporation in the world—except they operate outside of the law.

While gangsters continue to make staggering sums of money through such illegal activities as drug-smuggling, gambling, loan-sharking, and extortion, they also make a tidy profit when an ordinary, law-abiding citizen buys an ice cream cone or a slice of pizza, rides a taxicab, or joins a labor union. Organized crime is everywhere: mob activities pervade daily life in ways that most people never imagine.

The story of how the great gangsters battled for dominance among themselves and built their vast and powerful empires, and how crime-fighters tried to block their progress, is chronicled in this book.

Gambling was, and still is, a cornerstone of organized crime all over the world. Pictured above, a Havana casino in 1958.

CHAPTER ONE

THE MAFIA CONNECTION

Of the four English-speaking countries mentioned in the introduction, the United States is far and away the most significant hub of organized gang activity in the world. At the very heart of the multiethnic organized crime scene in the United States lie two elements: New York City and the Mafia. During Prohibition, the New York–based American Mafia expanded its control over an international crime empire, which today includes most of the United States, Canada, Australia, as well as other countries. Britain has largely escaped the tentacles of the American Mafia, but has developed its own homegrown gangsters, who have local influence and considerable wealth. Although the American Mafia's

Prohibition agents seize a stash of illegal liquor hidden beneath a huge pile of coal. Such successes hardly slowed the flow of liquor into the United States.

upper echelon is almost exclusively Sicilian, other members of today's Mafia are of various ethnic and national backgrounds.

In recent years, the American Mafia has lost its hold over the international crime scene. Ruthless drug cartels like the Colombian Medellin, highly organized Chinese triads, and Middle Eastern gangs in Chicago and Los Angeles have challenged the Mafia, making the international underworld far more fragmented than fifty or even fifteen years ago. Also, the Japanese yakuza has capitalized on Japan's international economic position to carve a growing empire.

Nevertheless, the American Mafiosi can still be considered the premier gangsters of the world.

The net profits for the American Mafia's U.S. operations alone total $30 billion each year. At the height of the Mafia's power, it was so wealthy and powerful that Meyer Lansky, the premier financial architect of this vast criminal empire, was said to have boasted: "We're bigger than U.S. Steel."

The Mafia originated in Sicily nearly one thousand years ago. Located southwest of Rome in the Mediterranean, the island of Sicily was repeatedly invaded by Arabs, Europeans, and bloodthirsty pirates. For hundreds of years Rome stood by and did nothing to protect the peasant farmers who inhabited Sicily. Treated like slaves by their conquerors and ignored by their fellow Italians, Sicilians turned inward, exhibiting a fierce independence and self-reliance. They came to believe that only fellow Sicilians, especially one's own family, could be trusted. The embittered Sicilians distrusted and feared the government, so they placed their faith in blood relatives. They never forgot that government was the enemy and that family honor was what truly mattered.

Out of the Sicilians' tenacious hatred for outsiders was formed a patriotic society that became known as the Mafia. The word "mafia" is of uncertain origin, but there are three credible possibili-

Beer being seized and destroyed in New York City, 1931. Alcohol was still produced in the United States during Prohibition, but only for medicinal uses.

ties. One version dates to the ninth century. The story is that Sicilian farmers fled to the hillsides to seek refuge from vicious Arab invaders, who referred to the runaways as mafia—meaning "place of refuge" in Arabic. Another story relates that in 1282 a French soldier raped a Sicilian girl in front of her mother who, torn with grief, ran through the cobblestone streets screaming, "Ma fia! Ma fia!" (my daughter!). At the town square she bemoaned the

loss of her family's honor and called for revenge; those who accepted her challenge adopted her cry. A third possibility is that the term "mafia" is an acronym of the famous Sicilian resistance motto, "Morte alla Francia Italia anele!" or, "Death to the French is Italy's cry!"

Despite the confusion surrounding the word's origin, one thing is certain: the Mafia was not originally a criminal society, but rather a patriotic one. However,

New York City's Little Italy during festival time. In major cities Italians bonded together to form tight communities.

by the nineteenth century the Mafia had been corrupted into a totally secret and powerful criminal society that ruled Sicily with an iron hand. The leaders of the patriotic Mafia, intoxicated with their power, had begun to use the society for their own benefit. Significantly, the ideals of unity, honor, and distrust of authority were carried on, but now in service of a fierce and virtually impregnable gang. The Mafia became an integral part of life in Sicily.

The southern Italian immigrants who settled in the bustling cities of the United States during the late nineteenth and early twentieth centuries brought with them the strong cultural traditions of the Mafia, and the lesser known Calabrian 'ndrangheta (Honored Society) and Neopolitan *Camorra*, two southern Italian criminal societies very much like the Mafia. In the Little Italy sections of New Orleans, New York, Chicago, and other big cities, the Sicilian Mafia underwent a metamorphosis that fused together ancient southern Italian traditions and modern American business methods to create a unique hybrid, which became known as the American Mafia or Cosa Nostra ("Our Thing"). The two individuals considered most responsible for forming the

American Mafia are Meyer Lansky and Lucky Luciano, whose stories will be told later.

The two ancient rules that the new American Mafia held most dear were *omerta* and obedience to superiors. Omerta, which means "noble silence," was a blood oath not to talk about the society to anyone, especially the authorities. Without omerta, secrecy was impossible; the society would be discovered and rooted out by the government. The rule of obedience ensured that the American Mafia could operate with military precision and a fairly rigid chain of command. These ancient traditions, combined with modern corporate strategies, make the American Mafia the giant that it is today.

Today, the overall organization of the American Mafia is widely known. Twenty-four separate criminal entities known as families rule territories throughout the United States and, in turn, indirectly control territories in Canada and Australia. At the head of each family is a *capo* ("boss"), who enjoys control over his family and territory. The boss, deferentially refered to as *don*, provides protection and political favors for his underlings in return for a cut of all action in his territory. In Mario Puzo's book *The Godfather*, Don Corleone is a popular, albeit fic-

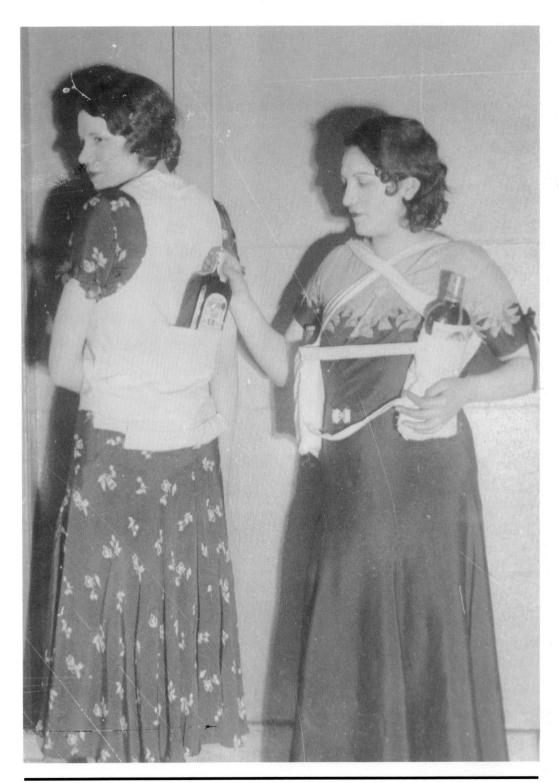

Smuggling liquor required ingenuity and daring. Here, two women show off their techniques for slipping by customs officials, 1931.

Marlon Brando and Al Pacino in The Godfather. *Brando's character, Don Corleone, is perhaps the most well-known celluloid mafia boss of all time.*

tional, example of a capo—the real-life gangster that Puzo based his character on was New York's Carlo Gambino.

With the advice of a *consigliere* ("counselor"), the boss issues instructions to trusted lieutenants or captains, called *caporegime*, who make sure that "soldiers" carry out his wishes. A smart boss never uses the telephone or any traceable form of communication to give orders but instead confides only in his most trusted lieutenants, who would deny that the boss ever issued such orders. Thus, bosses are insulated from the action on the streets and frequently avoid arrest because they are careful not to leave any traces.

The twenty-four families are overseen by a ruling "Commission" that handles all disputes between families, demarcates territory, and generally tries to keep unnecessary bloodshed to a minimum. However, murder will always be the ultimate threat to those who break the unwritten rules; as the mafiosi themselves say, "getting whacked" is the penalty for violating these rules.

Even though all twenty-four families participate in the Commission, the five New York families wield considerable influence. The New York Mafia has the largest membership and also controls the jewel of the criminal underworld—

Prohibition was an unpopular law that many thought encouraged crime instead of eliminating it. Thanks to such demonstrations as the women's march in Newark, New Jersey, shown above, Prohibition was eventually repealed in 1933.

New York City. With New York City as its headquarters, the American Mafia operates like a corporation with international clout.

The Mafia chooses it members carefully. Contrary to popular belief, being Sicilian is not a requirement, although rising to the top is unlikely if the man—membership is restricted to men—is not a full-blooded Sicilian. Automatic membership is often granted by birth or marriage. The membership process for a newcomer requires three phases. First, a candidate must demonstrate an early interest in crime and build enough of a reputation to attract the attention of a family. If the family decides to apprentice the would-be gangster, he must serve as a "soldier" for several years with a perfect record of omerta and obedience. The third and final phase occurs only if the boss decides the family needs new blood. If accepted as a full Mafiosi, the apprentice is "made" in a ceremony that is said to involve drawing blood from his gun finger, smearing a written oath with the blood, and then burning the piece of paper in the palm of his hand.

Once someone is admitted to the ranks of the Mafia, the only way out is through death.

CHAPTER TWO

UNITED STATES

Like no other country in the world, except perhaps Italy, the United States is fascinated, even mesmerized, by the mysterious ways of the Mafia and the great dons who supposedly run the underworld. Hollywood churns out smash hits like *The Godfather* trilogy, *Scarface, Goodfellas,* and a slew of others while the public voraciously devours each film and still has an appetite for more insider accounts of the Mafia. Although the media attention given to Italian gangsters might seem excessive, a close examination of the genesis of organized crime in America reveals that the Mafia deserves a special place. Not only is the Mafia the most powerful and enduring criminal organization in U.S. history, but it

Robert De Niro stars as Jimmy Conway in the movie Goodfellas. *Based on a true story, the film spans thirty years in the life of a Mafia family.*

has also produced some of the most flamboyant and vicious gangsters of all time. However, notorious Jewish and Irish gangsters also made major contributions to the rise of organized crime in the United States and should not be overlooked in favor of their Italian counterparts.

What might surprise some is that gangsters existed long before the Prohibition era. During the nineteenth century, simultaneous surges in industrial growth and foreign immigration transformed cities around the United States into buzzing hives of ethnic diversity and business activity. New Orleans, New York, and Chicago were the early centers of criminal activity where Jewish, Irish, and Italian gangs fought for suprem-

Unloading $500,000 worth of liquor to be burned by Prohibition agents. As the flames raged, a crowd gathered and looked on with mixed emotions.

acy. The stakes were small then, however, with small-time thugs usually battling for control of the various lucrative rackets within a neighborhood or at most throughout a small city. They stole, ran protection and gambling rackets, and otherwise milked money from their neighbors, but rarely posed any serious threat to society.

Originally, Italians with a mind for crime turned to plain and simple extortion, threatening neighborhood businessmen with violence unless they coughed up some cash. These "Black Handers," as they were known, delivered a note demanding a pay-off and signed the bottom with a hand-print in black ink (fingerprinting forced Black Handers to change this practice). The infamous Black Hand signature struck instant fear into any Old World Italian, bringing back memories of the *lupara*, the special sawed-off shotgun of the Sicilian Mafia. Black Hand targets almost always paid up because they knew that if they refused, violent retribution would follow. In New York, one Black Hander known as Lupo the Wolf widely publicized his "Murder Stable," where he had buried more than sixty people who had tried to avoid the grasp of the Black Hand.

The Mafia made its first appearance in New Orleans shortly after the Civil War. First limited to terrorizing Italian neighborhoods through Black Hand extortion, the budding Mafia began to look for more lucrative rackets. In the decades that followed, the Mafia muscled in on the protection racket at the ship-

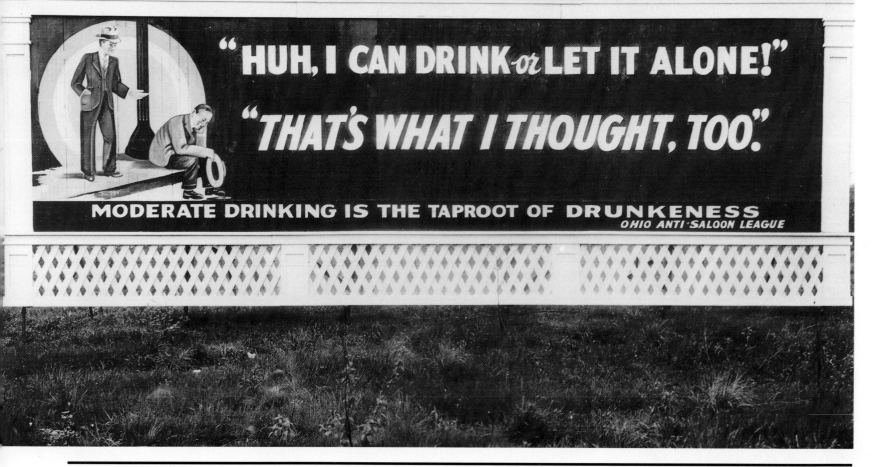

Support for Prohibition was strongest among women and Protestants. Many saw liquor as an evil that led to moral depravity.

ping docks, threatening violence unless they received a percentage of the profits. Violence erupted as the Mafia's efforts were resisted by the dockhands and the police.

David Hennessey, the New Orleans police chief, antagonized the Italians by refusing to back away from his investigation of the dock takeover. On October 15, 1890, Hennessey was walking home alone when he was ambushed by Mafia gunmen. After being hit with more than six gun blasts, Hennessey was found lying in the gutter. With his dying words, the chief of police implicated the Italians: "The dagoes [Italians]...they have given it to me...and I gave them back the best I could!"

The resulting flurry of public outrage against Italians led to a grand jury investigation, which announced to the nation that there had "developed the existence of the secret organization styled 'Mafia.'" Anti-Italian sentiment spun out of control in New Orleans and finally exploded when a mob of people took justice into its own hands and hanged suspected Italians from street posts. Tragically, some of the people dangling from the street posts had nothing to do with the Hennessey case, but all Italians were now suspected of being part of some dark, sinister criminal society.

Even after the New Orleans incident, the Mafia in the United States was little more than a disorganized, uncoordinated group of small-time gangs that terrorized the Italian neighborhoods of major cities. But things changed drastically on January 16, 1920—from then on organized crime would never be the same.

The Volstead Act, better known as Prohibition, became law on that fateful day. The Eighteenth Amendment of the U.S. Constitution clearly stated that "the manufacture, sale, or transportation of intoxicating liquors within, the importation thereof into, or the exportation thereof from the United States...is hereby prohibited." The United States became a dry country.

It is one of those ironies of history that the advocates of Prohibition believed that illegalizing alcohol would eradicate crime. The Anti-Saloon League and the Women's Christian Temperance Union fervently prophesied that stopping the flow of the devil's drink would also kill off other vices like prostitution and gambling. The supporters of Prohibition wanted to legislate morality, stop the decay of American society, and turn back the clock to a golden age of moral righteousness. Their plan backfired miserably.

Only thirty minutes after Prohibition went into effect, the first violation was reported—a trainload of whiskey had been hijacked. Gangsters quickly realized that the Volstead Act was both unpopular and unenforceable. Demonstrating more insight than the advocates of Prohibition, Irish, Italian, and Jewish gangs saw that the public's taste for alcoholic beverages would not vanish and that quenching that thirst would mean millions of dollars in tax-free income.

Bootlegging was considered little more than a public service. The mad rush to corner the bootlegging market brought rival gangs head-to-head and spawned some of the greatest gangster stories of all time.

ALPHONSE "SCARFACE" CAPONE

Al Capone was the archetypal Chicago gangster. During Prohibition, Capone made a fortune through bootlegging, bookmaking, and through houses of prostitution. At the pinnacle of his power, Capone was cheered at the ballpark while President Herbert Hoover was heckled. Capone received more fan mail than some Hollywood movie stars. But Al Capone's rise in the

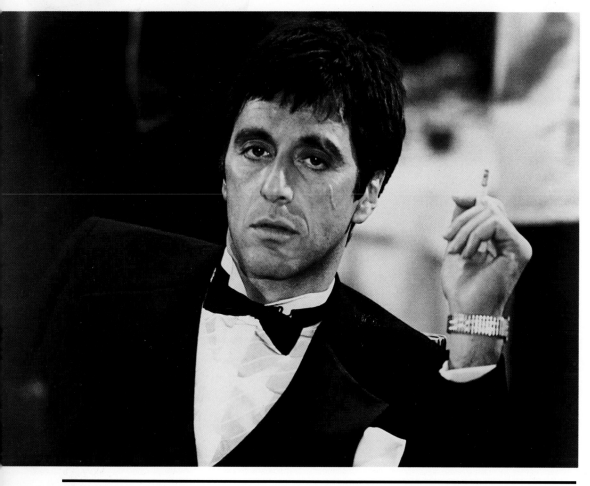

Al Pacino as a modern day Al Capone in Scarface. *For Pacino's character, cocaine, not alcohol, was the key to success.*

criminal underworld started long before Prohibition and far away from Chicago.

Capone was born on January 17, 1899, in Brooklyn, New York. He grew up on the Lower East Side of New York City, where he went to school with Charlie Luciano (Luciano went on to become a mastermind of the U.S. Mafia). Al made it to the sixth grade in school but only attended thirty-three of ninety school days in that semester, earning him a scolding from his teacher. Capone, upset with the teacher's attitude, slugged him in the face. The principal flogged Capone for bloodying the teacher's nose, and Capone never returned to school.

Out on the streets, Capone fell in with the older Johnny Torrio, who introduced the youngster to the criminal underworld. By his late teens, Capone was a member of the Five Points Gang, working as a bouncer at a Brooklyn saloon and whorehouse. At five-feet-ten (1.7 m) and 255 pounds (116 kg), Capone was built like a bull and he knew how to take care of himself. However, in one altercation, Capone's left cheek was slashed, thus earning him his nickname, "Scarface." Capone was extremely self-conscious about his wound; he covered his whole face with white talcum powder to hide the pink scar and always presented his right side to photographers. (Capone later hired the man who had slashed his face as his personal bodyguard in a rare act of forgiveness.)

By 1919 Capone had distinguished himself as a brawny street tough. However, he was not very subtle about his business and was a suspect in several murder cases. Torrio, now working in Chicago for "Big" Jim Colosimo, asked Capone to come to Chicago as his personal aide. Capone happily obliged, escaping the clutches of the New York authorities.

Capone was eager to make more money in Chicago so he could lavishly support his family. Torrio, who was Capone's mentor and confidant, quickly taught him about Colosimo's prostitution and gambling rackets in Chicago and suburban Cicero. Capone was getting his first experience as a manager rather than an enforcer, giving orders instead of taking them. Scarface was earning a nice living helping his old friend manage Colosimo's business.

When Prohibition hit, Torrio saw the potential profits and urged "Big" Jim to use his muscle to quickly monopolize the Chicago bootlegging scene before rival gangs could make a move. Colosimo—who was infatuated with a local nightclub singer and had his mind on love, not money—told Torrio he did not see why he should get into bootlegging. Torrio knew that his boss was going soft and, along with his protégé Capone, plotted the murder of "Big" Jim.

Colosimo was shot to death in front of his own restaurant by hired killer Frankie Yale. Everyone knew who was behind the killing, and Torrio quickly usurped Colosimo's power. Firmly in control, Torrio and Capone began a territorial expansion that included new bootlegging ventures. Torrio, a wise and visionary gangster, believed that peace was in everyone's interest, and so he desperately tried to avoid any further unnecessary gang violence. Bootlegging was soon the number-one money-maker for Torrio and Capone, who split the profits down the middle.

Ominously, all was not well in the Chicago underworld. The Irish

Al Capone, the king of the Chicago underworld who was renowned for his brutal punishments and tactics, in an uncharacteristic quiet moment.

Al Capone fishing on his boat.

severing the head would also kill the body of the O'Banionites. O'Banion was shot down in 1924 but a new boss, Hymie Weiss, quickly picked up the fight and swore revenge for O'Banion's murder.

On January 12, 1925, Weiss, hell-bent on vengeance, arranged a hit on Capone. Capone was injured in a drive-by shooting when his limousine was riddled with machine-gun fire. Capone, visibly distressed by his brush with death, ordered a custom-built, bulletproof Cadillac that weighed nearly seven tons (6.3 metric tons). Capone also ordered custom-made suits with rein-forced right pockets to support his revolver. His fear was so pro-found that he tried to take out a life insurance policy—but no company would cover him.

Torrio was also in great danger. In late 1925, Torrio pleaded guilty to a charge of operating a brewery because he thought he would be safer in jail than on the streets of Chicago. But before he made it to jail, he was shot up by Weiss's gang and barely survived. Tired and frightened, Torrio turned over the entire Chicago operation to the twenty-six-year-old Capone, saying, "Al, it's all yours."

Capone set up headquarters in a posh suite at the Hotel Met-ropole, complete with a full gym-

gangs of the North and South Sides were unhappy with the Italians' sudden move into boot-legging. The Irish dismissed Torrio's peace overtures and launched a counterattack that soon escalated into the most ferocious gang war in Chicago's history.

The main contender for the Italians' business was Dion O'Banion's North Side Gang. Hijacking the whiskey-laden trucks of Torrio and Capone, O'Banionites, as they were called, were causing serious problems. The Italian team decided that O'Banion had to go, hoping that nasium for his foot soldiers. In his office there were three portraits hanging over his desk—George Washington, Abraham Lincoln, and Chicago's mayor, "Big Bill" Thompson. Sitting behind his desk in his monogrammed silk pajamas, playing with his diamond pinky ring, Capone settled into his new position as undisputed head of the Chicago operation. He intensi-

fied his war with the remaining O'Banionites, who continued to be troublesome rivals.

Capone successfully had Weiss murdered on October 11, 1926, and thought he was rid of the Irish gang. Perhaps to celebrate his apparent victory, Capone paid a visit to his mistress, only to discover that she had contracted syphilis. His doctor urged him

to take a Wasserman test but, afraid of needles, Capone ignored the doctor's pleas—a decision he would later regret.

Returning to the battlefront, Capone discovered that his Irish adversaries refused to surrender; Bugs Moran had replaced Weiss and was ready to duke it out with Capone. Fed up with the fiesty Irish gang, Capone plotted

Kevin Costner as Eliot Ness in the 1987 film The Untouchables, *which portrays Ness' efforts to combat Capone in Prohibition era Chicago.*

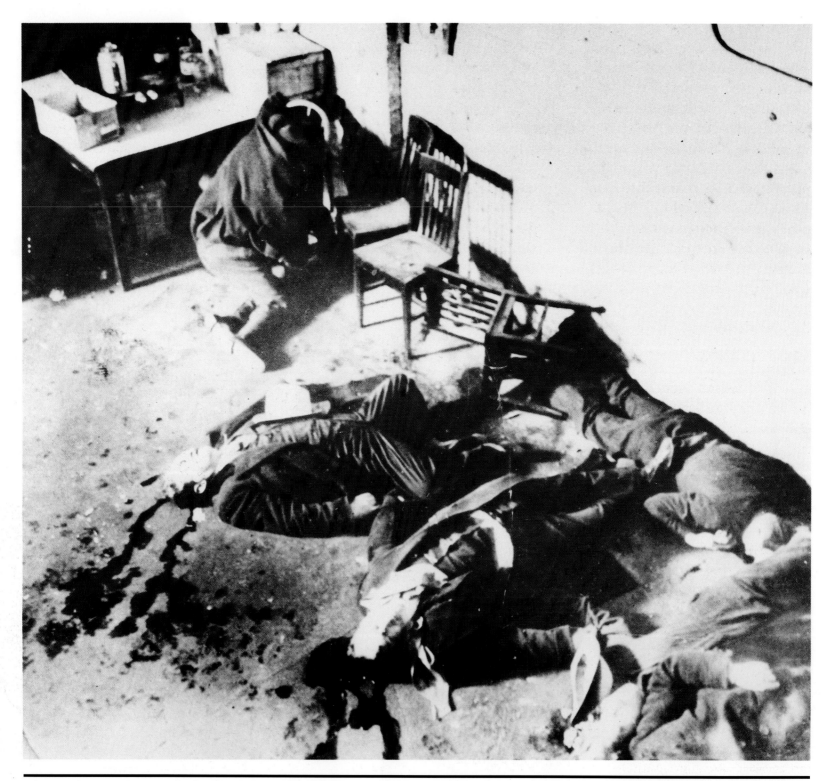

The bloody scene after the St. Valentine's Day Massacre. All seven bodies are not visible because one man crawled away from the wall, where he bled to death.

a wholesale massacre that would go down as one of the most notorious gang slayings of all time—the St. Valentine's Day Massacre.

On February 14, 1929, a police car pulled up to a warehouse at 2122 North Clark Street. Two uniformed officers and two plainclothesmen emerged from the car and entered the warehouse, where seven men were playing cards. Bugs Moran, who was on his way to the card game, had not yet arrived. The seven men, all part of Bugs Moran's gang, thought the cops were running a routine bust, so they did not object when the cops ordered them to face the wall and put their hands up. The cops and plainclothesmen then pulled out machine guns and shotguns and opened fire. Riddled with bullets, the seven men slumped to the ground and lay in a pool of blood that would eventually grow to cover forty square feet (3.6 sq m).

The four intruders who perpetrated the cold-blooded slayings were not policemen, but members of Capone's gang. Even though Moran himself was not at the card game, Capone had successfully wiped out enough of the O'Banionite leaders to be free of future challenges. However, the brutal and savage slayings appalled the public and attracted federal attention. Pushed by President Hoover,

federal authorities decided that the Chicago bootlegging wars had to end and that Capone must be put behind bars. The St. Valentine's Day Massacre, which Capone thought would finally make him king of Chicago, was actually the beginning of the end.

After the massacre, federal agents launched a two-pronged attack to land Capone in prison. The first strategy was to nail Capone for his bootlegging enterprises, which were in violation of

the Volstead Act. Eliot Ness was the agent who led this attack. The second strategy, which eventually put Capone in jail, was to charge him with income tax evasion—a good plan, considering Capone had never filed a tax return.

With the feds on his tail, Capone suspected his underlings of plotting his demise. He believed that three of his henchmen—Hop Toad Giunta, John Scalise, and Albert Anselmi—were showing signs of disloyalty, which Capone

A view of Alcatraz from the rear as it would have appeared to Capone in 1934.

loathed. He decided to make an example of the trio. Capone invited the three "traitors" to a dinner party in their honor and served magnificent food washed down with gallons of red wine. After all the dinner guests were stuffed, Capone's mood suddenly turned sour and he rose from his chair, approached the three men with a baseball bat in his hands, and mercilessly pulverized their skulls for all to see. Capone's message was perfectly clear—he was not to be crossed.

But Capone's future looked dismal as the Internal Revenue Service closed in on him. While Eliot Ness was meeting with limited success, the IRS put together a strong case and took Capone to court. As the city of Chicago looked on, a guilty verdict was handed down and the legendary Chicago gangster was sentenced to eleven years at the federal penitentiary in Atlanta.

In 1934, Capone was transferred to Alcatraz, in San Francisco Bay, where advanced syphilis ravaged his brain. Capone was never a force in the underworld again. He was released in 1939 so he could live out the rest of his life near his family in Florida. In an unglamorous end, Alphonse Capone drifted in and out of a vegetative state until he died on January 25, 1947.

Meyer Lansky being booked in 1958. Lansky, actively involved in introducing modern business practices to the Mafia, was frequently booked, but never convicted.

THE LANSKY-LUCIANO GANG

One particular meeting on a snow-covered street on the Lower East Side of Manhattan was the beginning of a partnership that would totally transform organized crime in America and beyond. In 1914 or 1915 a lone Jewish boy was walking on the sidewalk, his thoughts on trivial matters. He did not notice the gang of Italian thugs that was walking toward him until it was too late. They surrounded him, and then the leader, with menace in his voice, said, "If you wanna keep alive, Jew boy, you gotta pay us five cents a week protection money...." The young boy, outnumbered and smaller than the smallest of the Italians, glared at the leader and answered, "Go f- - - yourself."

Charlie Luciano, the leader of the gang, impressed by the boy's courage, prevented his friends from beating Meyer Lansky to a pulp. Even though it was the first time they met, Luciano took an immediate liking to this "Little Man" who would fight against such odds. They were a perfect match. Lansky would grow to be a quiet man with an ingenious financial mind who preferred to work behind the scenes but would never shy from necessary confrontation. Luciano was loud,

Lucky Luciano (seen here in Italy after being deported from the United States) was the first mafioso to wield national power.

Bugsy Siegel, Lansky's closest friend, was a notorious ladies' man. He was given his nickname, however, for his crazy outbursts of physical violence.

boisterous, and commanded immense respect in the Italian community. In the years that followed, Charlie Luciano and Meyer Lansky grew closer than brothers and eventually sky-rocketed to the very top of the gangster world.

Meyer Lansky loved America. He was so taken with the country that when he immigrated to the United States from Grodno, Poland, in 1911, he claimed that his birthday was July 4. As a youngster on the Lower East Side, his first love was not school, not girls, but gambling. Studying the card and dice games that took place on virtually every street, Lansky realized that the only people who really ended up winning were the Italians who ran the operations. After graduating from eighth grade, Lansky took a job at a tool-and-die factory but decided that his real future would be in gambling.

Lansky built a gang of tough Jewish mobsters to carry out his dream. Bugsy Siegel was his right-hand man. Loyal, fiesty, violent, and prone to use his gun before his brain, Siegel was at different times Lansky's greatest asset and liability. The "Bug and Meyer" gang established a strong reputation for conducting a clean and efficient business. However, there was a limit to how far Lansky could go, because the old Italian dons still wielded considerable power in New York.

All the while, Luciano was busy building his own gang. He chose Frank Costello as his right-hand man and enlisted people like Vito Genovese, Carlo Gambino, and Albert Anastasia—a veritable who's who of future leaders of the Mafia. Luciano was successful but suffered from the same problem as Lansky: the old Italians, or "Mustache Petes," were always hovering over his head.

In an attempt to solve the Mustache Pete problem, Lansky and Luciano merged their respective gangs into the Lansky-Luciano gang. These two upstarts successfully turned the protection rackets and gambling operations on the Lower East Side into major money-making scams and, at Lansky's suggestion, they stashed the profits for later investments. Still, the specter of the more powerful, entrenched gangs meant their future was uncertain.

The Lansky-Luciano gang was threatened in 1919 when Joe Masseria, one of the old Italians, began cracking heads on the Lower East Side. Masseria had decided that the Lansky-Luciano gang was infringing on his territory and therefore must pay him tribute. Realizing they were up against a powerful foe, the

Jewish-Italian team struck back at the aging Masseria. The gamble payed off as Masseria backed away from a full-scale war. Masseria and the other Mustache Petes had suffered a setback. But this was only the beginning of what eventually became the Castellammarese War, when the "Young Turks" finally dethroned the Mustache Petes.

The only thing that stopped Lansky and Luciano from pressing Masseria at the time was the beginning of Prohibition. They realized that their energies could be better spent in getting into the bootlegging business rather than engaging in a long, protracted war. Luckily for them, the duo was approached by the world-renowned, high-class gambler Arnold Rothstein. Rothstein, the man credited with bribing eight of nine baseball players in the 1919 Chicago Black Sox scandal, proposed a partnership with Lansky and Luciano. If they could gain access to the best European Scotch Whiskey, Rothstein suggested that there was a wealthy clientele who would pay outrageous prices for the liquor. Rothstein would handle the European end, shipping the whiskey within the legal three miles (4.8 km) of U.S. shores. Then Lansky and Luciano would arrange to meet the ships, transport the

whiskey the three miles to shore, and sell the fine whiskey to high-society buyers.

The setup was a runaway success. While their competitors had low-grade moonshine that could cause blindness or death, the Lower East Side operation provided the finest whiskey to discerning palates. The job of protecting the whiskey transports fell to Italians like Joe Adonis, Vito Genovese, and Carlo Gambino, but Lansky and Luciano were not above riding shotgun on important shipments. For a while, gang conflict was minimal in comparison to the battles raging in Chicago.

Lansky, reading book after book on business finance, applied new techniques to the bootlegging enterprise, increasing their profits. Luciano, who always enjoyed public attention, was rubbing elbows with high-society figures, constantly bringing in new customers, and rapidly gaining a reputation as a powerful gangster. In another odd twist of history, bootlegging actually gave gangsters legitimacy and respect because nobody really thought of selling or drinking alcohol as a serious crime.

The wholly improbable Jewish-Italian bootlegging team totally outmaneuvered the old Mustache Petes, especially their old enemy, don Masseria, and the ambitious

Frank Costello, Luciano's advisor, moved up in the criminal underworld after Luciano's deportation.

don Salvatore Maranzano. The situation was explosive, and the old-timers, who had been slow to see the potential of bootlegging, tried to muscle in on Lansky and Luciano. On October 17, 1929, Luciano, without consulting Lansky, went alone to a deserted garage on Staten Island to talk peace with Maranzano. Peace was not what Maranzano had in mind—he had Luciano beaten and his face slashed, telling him that he must kill Masseria, then cut loose from the Jewish gang and serve under the great don Maranzano.

When a patrol car found Luciano on the side of the road, the officers thought he was dead. He was rushed to a hospital where he miraculously recovered from his beating. At three in the morning Lansky and his friends arrived. Lansky, furious with Luciano for going to the meeting alone, told his old friend that he was lucky to be alive. From that point on, "Lucky" was the nickname that would stick with Luciano until his death.

The pair now planned revenge against Maranzano. Luciano had already been planning to kill Masseria before this incident so he went ahead with the hit and made it seem as if he was following the orders of Maranzano. Maranzano consequently appointed himself "the boss of all bosses" in an elaborate gala event. He also organized a commission of the ruling families, with himself at the head and Luciano at his side.

Even with this apparent success, Maranzano remained wary of his partners, suspecting them of plotting his assassination. He was very careful around all Italians. But, despite his cautiousness, Lansky and Luciano were able to concoct an ingenious plan to kill Maranzano in his Park Avenue office. IRS agents often dropped by unannounced to look over Maranzano's books, so he thought nothing of it when four Jewish men, posing as IRS agents, knocked at his door on September 10, 1931. Suspecting nothing more than financial harassment (Maranzano was hopelessly anti-Semitic), he allowed them into his office. The imposters pulled their revolvers, tied up his bodyguards, and then stabbed Maranzano repeatedly, pumping six bullets into his heart for insurance.

With this coup de grace, the dynamic duo was poised to take over the New York crime world and usher in the modern era of the American Mafia. Lansky and the Jewish contingent continued to operate behind the scenes, and the mafiosi, many of whom were anti-Semitic, saw Luciano as the man to be reckoned with. In a rare

Luciano was such a celebrity that the paparazzi went to great lengths to catch him in unguarded moments like this.

move, Luciano turned down the position of boss of all bosses, also refusing to accept cash tributes from the other families. Instead, Luciano talked of a new era, a time when old Sicilian jealousy would be put to rest and peace would reign. Cooperation, not feuding, would ensure profit for all. Lucky, mouthing the ideas he and Lansky had worked out, suggested that there was more than enough money and power to go around for all the families. The true American Mafia was born.

The younger gangsters loved the ideas of increased upward mobility and greater shared profits, but some of the veterans were slow to give up the old ways. However, the plan was so brilliant that all of the families' profits went up, while the bloodshed slowed to a trickle. One Lansky gang member was so impressed with the duo's managerial skills that he believed, "If they had become president and vice president of the United States they would have run the place far better than the idiot politicians that did it."

The thirties started off fantastically. Sensing that Prohibition would not last, Lansky and Luciano expanded their gambling operations. In partnership with Frank Erickson (Arnold Rothstein's successor) and the communications giant Moses

Annenberg, they created a nationwide off-track betting empire that allowed bookmakers to lay off large bets and skim profits for the gangsters who protected the illegal gambling. Lansky, who was always looking to the future, visited Cuba and befriended the dictatorial president Zaldívar y Batista, hoping to build casinos near the fine beaches of Havana. Lansky also had his eye on Las Vegas, which was at that time nothing more than a desert stopover.

However, the decade was not all smooth sailing for Lansky and Luciano. The political climate had changed; America was less hospitable to gangsters after the repeal of Prohibition in 1933 and the election of Franklin Roosevelt in 1932. Spearheading a new attack on gangsters was Thomas Dewey, the U.S. attorney for the southern district of New York and later governor of New York. Dewey pursued Luciano with a vengeance and succeeded in charging the racketeer with running a prostitution ring in 1936. Luciano fled to a gangster resort in Hot Springs, Arkansas, but was extradited to New York to face the charges. Facing a hostile judge, a prejudiced jury, and witnesses who gave coerced testimony (one prostitute said she slept with Lucky and he was unable to perform),

Luciano was convicted and sentenced to an unprecedented thirty to fifty years in prison.

The stiff penalty was not the end of Luciano; he still wielded considerable strength and respect in the underworld scene from his jail cell at Dannemora, New York. But now Lansky had to take a more active and public role in masterminding their operations. Luciano, in an act that shows just how much he trusted the "Little Man," turned over all his financial dealings to Lansky. With Luciano's display of trust, the rest of the Mafia were forced to accept the fact that their de facto leader was a Jew.

Lansky and Luciano continued to build their empire, especially in Las Vegas, Florida, and Cuba. After a rocky start, in the late thirties, hotel casinos in Las Vegas began to flourish. The Cuban Hotel Nacional, hailed as the most luxurious resort in the world, opened in Havana in 1937. Lansky was pursuing his childhood dream—gambling.

When the United States entered World War II in 1941, Luciano had an unusual opportunity to serve his country from jail. After the debacle of Pearl Harbor, the Navy was worried about security in New York Harbor. On November 9, 1942, the *Normandie* went up in flames while docked in New

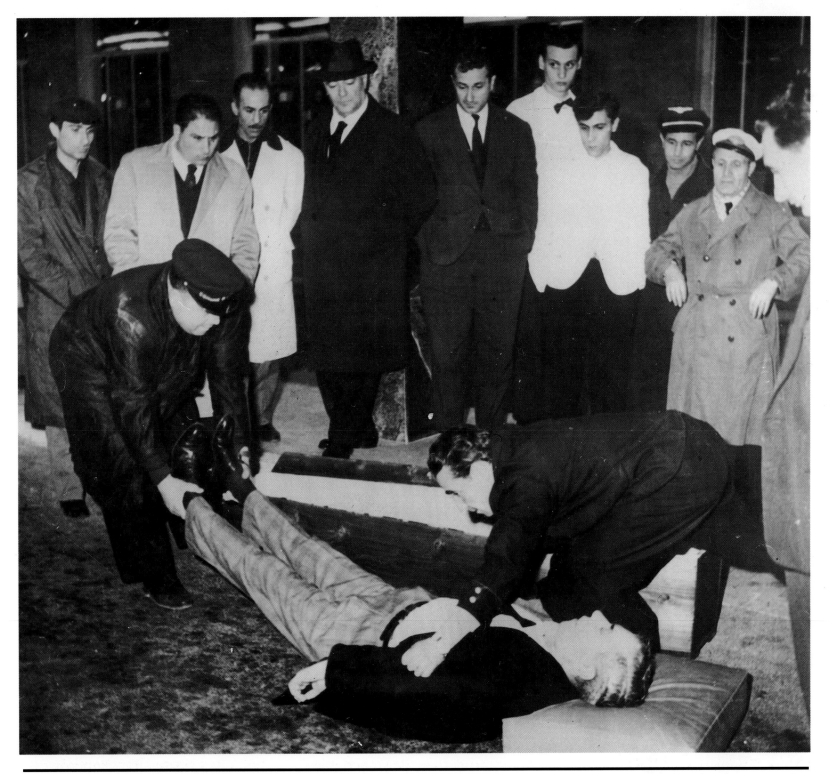

Lucky Luciano lying dead at Naples Airport in 1964. The fact that he died of natural causes was a testament to the respect he commanded.

York; the suspected cause was sabotage. Commander Haffenden, a Naval intelligence officer, approached Luciano with a deal. The Commander knew that Luciano controlled the dockhand unions and asked Luciano to use his clout to order an all-out vigilance campaign. In return, Haffenden guaranteed a commutation of Luciano's sentence. Luciano accepted the deal and lived up to his end of the bargain.

When the war ended, the Navy completely denied that it had ever struck any bargain with the Mafia. However, the evidence was so overwhelmingly in Luciano's favor that the Governor of New York, Thomas Dewey (the man who had put Luciano behind bars), issued a pardon, saying, "Luciano's aid to the Navy in the war was extensive and valuable." Dewey's powers were limited, though, so he could not prevent the revoking of Luciano's citizenship and his subsequent exile to Italy. In a grand send-off, Luciano said farewell to his longtime partner.

Lansky still visited his friend in Italy and they met on occasion at the Hotel Nacional in Havana. (Lansky went to great lengths to bring Lucky's favorite singer, Frank Sinatra, to the Nacional.) Luciano, however, was distant from the center of power and

therefore lost much of his prior prestige. For nineteen long years, Luciano struggled with his new position until he finally died of a heart attack at the Naples airport in 1964.

Lansky had to continue his criminal empire-building without another old friend, Bugsy Siegel. Right before Luciano died, Lansky painfully watched as Siegel dug his own grave. Siegel, always a ladies' man, had fallen under the spell of Virginia Hill, the "Mistress of the Mob." While overseeing the Las Vegas operations, Siegel had been skimming money off the top and sending his girlfriend to Switzerland, where she was seen depositing the money into a Swiss bank account. Informers let Lansky know about his old friend's thievery, giving Lansky a chance to talk some sense into the love-struck Siegel. Unfortunately, the talking did no good—Siegel was hopelessly spellbound by Hill. Lansky finally agreed that Siegel had to be "put to sleep."

Although Lansky was now without his closest conspirators, he steadfastly held on to the reigns of organized crime throughout the fifties and sixties. During the late sixties, however, Lansky came under federal investigation for his numerous illegal activities and for the Achilles' heel of gangsters everywhere: tax evasion.

Hassled by federal authorities, Lansky was having a very difficult time managing his empire.

Trying to avoid the wrath of U.S. authorities, Lansky fled to Israel in 1970, where he applied for citizenship. However, after pressing his case for twenty-six months, Lansky was denied citizenship; the highest court of Israel ruled that Lansky was "a danger to public safety," even though he had not been convicted of a major crime since the thirties. Dismayed that the Jewish state had refused his request, Meyer Lansky was a man without a country.

Although the Israeli government denied Lansky's pleas for citizenship, he was issued an Israeli passport because his U.S. passport was invalid for all destinations except the United States. The Israelis' gesture made no difference—seven countries refused Lansky's $1 million cash offer for sanctuary and he had no choice but to return to the United States.

On November 7, 1972, Lansky touched American soil and was arrested immediately. The "Little Man" had this to say upon his arrest: "That's life. At my age, it's too late to worry. What will be will be. A Jew has a slim chance in the world." Lansky was being overly pessimistic—he beat, or was judged too ill to face, all of the charges against him. Lansky died a free man at the age of eighty-one in Miami Beach, Florida, with nearly $300 million stashed away in Swiss bank accounts.

A GALLERY OF GREAT AMERICAN GANGSTERS

Tony "Joe Batters" Accardo

"Joe Batters" served under Al Capone in Chicago, where he was known for his proficient use of the baseball bat as a tool of persuasion. Accardo eventually took over Capone's gang, but he never lost his touch with the baseball bat. For example, when he discovered that his underling "Action" Jackson was stealing from him, Accardo had Jackson strung up on a meat hook and then began batting practice on his testicles. To make a good example of Jackson, Accardo then ordered two days of torture. Jackson's eyes were burnt out with a blow torch, his body racked with electric shocks and then carved with a razor blade; the coroner determined that Jackson had died from the shock of the experience, not from the wounds sustained during the ordeal.

Louis "Two Gun" Alterie

Alterie was a psychopathic Irishman who worshiped Dion O'Banion. Originally from a ranch in Colorado, he boasted of his perfect marksmanship with both hands, and he shot out more than a few saloon lights to prove his point. His exploits earned him his Chicago nickname, "Two Gun." When O'Banion was gunned down by Capone's men, Alterie went on a rampage and publicly announced that "all twelve bullets in these rods have Capone's initials carved on their noses." His careless remark cost him his life when he was finally put to rest at Capone's order in 1935.

Virginia "Mistress of the Mob" Hill

Hill shared her bed with such Mafia greats as Joe Adonis, Frank Costello, Bugsy Siegel, and Al Capone's tax expert, Joe Epstein. Epstein once said of Hill, "Once that girl is under your skin, it's like a cancer. It's incurable." When Hill herself was asked to explain her popularity with gangsters,

Virginia Hill was known for throwing lavish parties.

she modestly explained that she was the "best goddam lay in the country."

Owney "The Killer" Madden

Madden earned his nickname during his early years in New York's Hell's Kitchen, where he was arrested forty-four times for suspected murder. A rare white Protestant in a mostly ethnic criminal scene, Madden retired from New York to run a gangster resort in Hot Springs, Arkansas. He married the postmaster's daughter and died a respected citizen of the small town.

Frank Sinatra

Frank Sinatra is one of the most famous and respected entertainers in the world. He is also a man with close ties to the Mafia, an association that continues to cause him great embarrassment. Sinatra's alleged Mafia connections inspired Mario Puzo, author of *The Godfather*, to base the character Johnny Fontaine on Sinatra's life story; for anyone who has read *The Godfather* or seen the movie, it might seem as if you have heard Sinatra's story before.

Sinatra was going nowhere as a young nightclub singer in New Jersey until he met Willie Moretti,

an extortionist, drug trafficker, and murderer. Moretti enjoyed Sinatra's act, so he helped him book performances at hot nightclub spots. Moretti's help gave Sinatra the exposure he desperately needed.

In 1939, Sinatra recorded his first hit, "All or Nothing at All." His success caught the attention of Tommy Dorsey, who signed Sinatra to a modestly generous contract. Soon after signing, Sinatra's career skyrocketed but Dorsey would not release him from the contract. Frustrated and angry that Dorsey would not release him, Sinatra called on his

Frank Sinatra, pictured here with Carlo Gambino, Jimmy Fratianno, and other mafiosi, has been plagued by this photo since it was taken in 1976.

old friend Willie Moretti. Moretti persuaded Dorsey to release Sinatra in exchange for one dollar. Apparently Moretti made Dorsey "an offer that he couldn't refuse."

Sinatra was indebted to many mobsters and over the years he has been photographed with such notorious gangsters as Lucky Luciano, Carlo Gambino, and Jimmy Fratianno. During the forties, he often performed at special Mafia occasions. In the early sixties, Robert Kennedy banned Sinatra from the White House because of his underworld affiliations. In more recent years, Sinatra has been very careful to keep his connections to the underworld private.

Joseph Kennedy

The Kennedy family is perhaps one of the best-known and most influential families in the United States. Although the Kennedys are usually known for their political exploits, little is said about their underworld connections. But the Kennedy family's history is riddled with shady dealings and political intrigue.

Joseph Kennedy, the patriarch of the family, was a ruthless businessman who made his fortune as a bootlegger during Prohibition. After Prohibition ended, Kennedy turned his attention to more legitimate business practices, but he

Joe Kennedy, Sr. with John (left) and Joe, Jr. (right). The most prominent political family of the twentieth century gained its wealth through organized crime during Prohibition.

never lost touch with his underworld friends and he continued to call on these powerful connections his whole life.

Kennedy was able to earn a reputation as an upstanding citizen of the United States and eventually served as ambassador to Great Britain during World War II. However, by publicly insisting that the United States should not aid the Allies during the war, he killed his own political career and was forced to abandon his presidential aspirations. But Kennedy kept his sights on the White House: he wanted his children to have the political career that he could no longer have. After his first son, Joe, was killed in 1944, Kennedy groomed John for the presidency. And as the 1960 election approached, Kennedy called on his underworld friends to use their muscle to swing the urban vote toward his son, who defeated Richard Nixon in one of the closest elections in U.S. history.

The mobsters, having helped put JFK into office, expected the president to return the favor by relaxing federal pressure on organized crime. However, JFK did exactly the opposite when he appointed his brother Robert as attorney general, who launched an all-out attack on organized crime.

Many historians believe that the Mafia was so angry with JFK for his betrayal that a contract was put out on his life. Indeed, there is mounting evidence that certain mobsters may have been responsible for the assassination of JFK on November 22, 1963.

Moses Annenberg

Born in 1878, "Moe" Annenberg grew up in poverty on the South Side of Chicago. Starting out as a struggling newspaper-circulation man, Annenberg eventually rose to the number-one circulation position for Hearst Publications. His circulation tactics were quite unorthodox: his band of toughs would overturn competitors' trucks, burn their papers, and beat up vendors. By 1926, Annenberg quit Hearst's employ to pursue his own business. He hit the jackpot when he and Frank Erickson, a close associate of Lansky and Luciano, formed the Nation-Wide News Service. The service illegally supplied racetrack information to bookmakers in 223

cities via wire and telephone; Moe was AT&T's fifth biggest customer. With the profits from Nation-Wide, Annenberg built a massive communications empire.

In 1939, Moe and his son Walter were charged with large-scale income tax evasion. Moe took the rap so his son could go free. Walter continued to expand his father's communications empire and went on to become a respected and prominent (not to mention affluent) U.S. citizen; he also eventually served as ambassador to England under Richard Nixon.

Albert Anastasia.

Santos Trafficante's gambling casino in Havana. Trafficante was wanted for questioning concerning Albert Anastasia's murder.

Joe Adonis

Joe's real last name was Doto, but he changed it to Adonis because of his self-proclaimed good looks. He served under Luciano in the early years and was one of the gunmen who killed Joe Masseria. He went on to control Brooklyn and run a famous restaurant that doubled as a meeting place for mobsters and politicians alike.

Albert "The Mad Hatter" Anastasia

Like so many of the great Mafia figures, Anastasia got his start in the Luciano operation. He became head of Murder, Inc., which was the execution squad for the Mafia. As a boss, he was too fond of killing as a means of solving his problems. His penchant for murder eventually caught up with him on October 25, 1957, when he was shot to death in the barbershop of the Park Sheraton Hotel in New York City.

Vincent "Mad Dog" Coll

In the early thirties, "Mad Dog" Coll was known as the quintessential Irish gangster gone crazy. He totally ignored the emerging Italian hold on organized crime and launched his own one-man terror campaign. He thought violence could get him anything he wanted and even tried to kill top members of the Mafia. In one

Vincent Coll (far right) and his gang after being arrested for the murder of a five-year-old child.

attack, he mowed down five children, killing a five-year old, but missed his target. Even though the famous criminal lawyer Sam Leibowitz got him off for the child's murder, mob justice caught up with Coll on Feb 9, 1932, in a phone booth, where he was mowed down by machine-gun fire.

Joe "Bananas" Bonanno

Leader of one of the five New York families during the thirties, forties, and fifties, Bonanno's ultimate ambition was to be boss of all bosses. To this end, he took out contracts on Carlo Gambino

and Tommy Lucchese, two prominent Mafia figures. His plan was discovered, and a small war ensued, leading to Bonanno's semi-retirement in Arizona. Yet Bonanno, even from Arizona, had significant control over the Canadian crime scene. Bonanno is still alive today, but his influence has dwindled in his old age.

Jimmy Hoffa

This famous Teamsters Union leader was deeply involved with organized crime. He stole from union funds and worked with the U.S. Mafia to control labor disputes. In the early sixties, Robert

After spending 4 years and 9 months behind bars, Jimmy Hoffa petitioned for prison reforms before he mysteriously disappeared.

Carmine "The Cigar Problem" Galante

Released from prison in 1974 after doing twelve years for drug trafficking, Galante tried to shoot his way back to the top of the Mafia scene. Noted for always having a cigar in his mouth, he and his gang went on a shooting spree that greatly upset the ruling families, who finally decided to have him "put to sleep" on July 12, 1979. After finishing his main course at Joe and Mary's Restaurant, Galante had just popped a cigar in his mouth when his assassins emerged and shot him to death. His cigar was still lit when the police arrived.

John "The Dapper Don" Gotti

John Gotti has been considered the top New York Mafia don since the mid-to-late eighties. Gotti's meteoric rise began in the sixties when he was a mere street punk with a flair for violence. His big break as a mobster came in 1973, when Gotti earned the admiration of Carlo Gambino for murdering James McBratney, the man who had kidnapped and murdered Carlo Gambino's son. However, Gotti lost his benefactor when Gambino died in his sleep in 1976.

Gambino's hand-picked successor was Paul Castellano, an

Kennedy put Hoffa behind bars. After his release Hoffa tried to regain control of the union. The Mafia tried to dissuade Hoffa from his comeback because they felt his image was too tainted. Hoffa refused to listen to his old partners and mysteriously disappeared on July 30, 1970. Although the mystery has never been solved, the most plausible explanation is that Hoffa was killed by the Mafia and his body run through a fat-rendering plant.

Leroy "Nicky" Barnes

Barnes was born in Harlem in 1933 and made his fortune as a narcotics racketeer for the Mafia. He loved to show off his wealth, driving around in either his Mercedes or his Maserati while carrying huge sums of money in his trunk. He was finally caught in 1978 and accused of dealing more than 40 pounds (18.2 kg) of heroin per month from a Harlem garage. He was sentenced to life in prison.

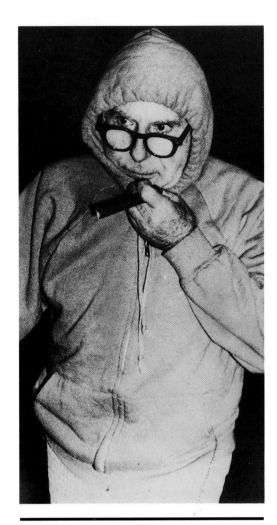

Carmine Galante rushing to Newark Airport after being released from prison.

he was arrested and charged with attempted murder in January 1989. But Gotti was not easily daunted by anyone, much less the government. When he saw the evidence against him, he brazenly declared, "Three-to-one odds I beat this case."

Indeed, with the help of his ace attorney, Bruce Cutler, Gotti beat the charges and was subsequently able to win two other cases brought against him. Of late, Gotti has not been so fortunate. He recently faced his fourth indictment—without the assistance of Bruce Cutler, who was deemed "too involved" with the charges under consideration to provide worthwhile counsel—and was found guilty on murder and racketeering charges. It seems that the Dapper Don will be wearing pinstripes for a long time; he was sentenced to life imprisonment with no chance for parole.

unpopular choice with the rest of the Gambino family. Gotti, in particular, felt that Castellano was allowing the great Gambino family to wither away. In 1985, Gotti had Castellano bumped off and took the reigns of the Gambino family in an attempt to regain the glory days. Gotti ruled with an iron hand for four years and greatly restored the family's image until

John Gotti in Manhattan's State Supreme Court in 1990. He was declared not guilty.

CHAPTER THREE

CANADA

Johnny Papalia, gambler and underworld figure of Hamilton, Ontario, was also heavily involved in a New York narcotics racket during the early 1960s.

The gangsters of Canada have legendary reputations for being suave and diplomatic. In fact, Vic "The Egg" Cotroni, the Godfather of Montreal for most of the twentieth century, was renowned for his modesty and mediating skills. However, even the diplomatic Cotroni was not above murdering competition if there was no alternative. He died of natural causes in 1984—a rare privilege in a dangerous profession.

Canadian characters like Cotroni, Rocco Perri, and Johnny "Paps" Papalia, despite being more refined than their U.S. counterparts, were dependent on, even controlled by, the unruly Mafia families of New York. During the Prohibition years, gangsters operating in the United States forged strong business relationships with Canadian bootleggers. Eventually the U. S. Mafia came to dominate, at least indirectly, the Canadian underworld.

The Prohibition years were a formative time for Canadian gangsters. Like their U.S. counterparts, Canadian gangsters had been involved in a number of small-time extortion rackets, which brought in modest profits throughout the early twentieth century. But when the American Prohibition experiment went into effect in 1920, Canadian gangsters entered the bootlegging business with a vengeance.

During Prohibition, Canadian bootleggers took advantage of the fact that there was no law against manufacturing liquor in Canada. Although alcohol consumption did decrease in the twenties, Canadian alcohol manufacturers were not hampered by any national prohibition laws.

Canadian bootlegging operations. Perri became so proficient at increasing the reliable flow of liquor into the United States that he was crowned the "king of the bootleggers" and was sometimes refered to as "Canada's Al Capone." Perri, more than any other Canadian gangster, put the Canadian crime world on the map.

Like so many other Italian gangsters, he got his start in the Little Italy of a major city (in this case Hamilton, Ontario). By 1916, the young Perri was heavily involved in Black Hand extortion

Rocco Perri, the self-styled "king of bootleggers in Hamilton," and two companions miraculously survived the explosion that demolished his car when he stepped on the starter, triggering a concealed bomb.

Consequently, for Canadian breweries and distilleries, January 16, 1920, was a godsend; they began churning out liquor to supply the black market. The only possible problem was exporting the liquor into the United States, a direct violation of the Volstead Act.

PROHIBITION AND ROCCO PERRI

Smuggling liquor into the United States was actually a relatively risk-free business. The automobile, which was in widespread use by this time, was the perfect bootlegging transport because of its size and mobility. Also, the undefended long border between Canada and the United States was, and still is very difficult to patrol. For Canadian gangsters, the chances of getting caught were overshadowed by the profits that could be made by selling cheap, tax-free Canadian liquor for outrageous prices on the black market in the United States.

The situation was ripe for an organized gang to go into the bootlegging business. Rocco Perri, seeing his big chance, started one of the first and most important

Rocco Perri at Toronto's Union Station in 1939. Perri was on his way to Windsor to stand trial for corrupting Canadian customs officials.

in the Hamilton area. Never an advocate of violence, Perri's early experiences confirmed his belief that unnecessary violence hurt business and was therefore an unsound practice. During his tenure as a Black Hander in the late 1910s, a flurry of bombings ripped through the Simcoe Street area of Hamilton, leaving whole families crushed to death in their own homes. Local newspapers ran stories about the Simcoe Street bombings with headlines like "Terror Reigns Amongst Italians." These horror-filled days left a deep mark on Perri—he swore to use diplomacy and efficiency rather than terror tactics if he ever came to power.

Perri's opportunity for achieving power and wealth came when Prohibition hit just across the border. Although still struggling to maintain his autonomy from the burgeoning U.S. Mafia, Perri supplied the market with huge amounts of liquor. While helping to quench a nation's thirst, Perri amassed a fortune and quickly diversified his operations to include gambling and protection rackets. As he had vowed to do back in the days of the Simcoe Street bombings, Perri ran his new gang with both efficiency and diplomacy.

Despite his relatively peaceful control of Hamilton, Perri had a difficult time maintaining his power after Prohibition ended in 1933. During the prior thirteen years, he had had something that people wanted and couldn't get elsewhere. But as soon as Prohibition was repealed, characters like Rocco Perri lost a major source of income and power. In addition, U.S. mafiosi, no longer dependent on Canadian liquor suppliers, made concerted efforts to bring Canadian cities within their grasp during the thirties and forties. Perri, however, was able to hold on to his control of Hamilton until his death in 1944.

VIC "THE EGG" COTRONI

After Rocco Perri's death, the New York families intensified their efforts to bring Canada into their sphere of influence. The most durable and lucrative link between the Canadian and the U.S. underworld existed between Montreal's Vic "The Egg" Cotroni and the Bonanno family of Buffalo, New York. Their relationship spanned three decades, but eventually faltered in the 1980s, throwing the Canadian underworld into chaos.

Vincenzo Cotroni was born in southern Italy and immigrated to Montreal with his parents in 1924. His parents, Nicodemo

Vic Cotroni, the Godfather of Montreal during the fifties, sixties, and seventies, remained in power for a long time thanks to his diplomacy.

and Maria, moved into an apartment at the corner of Ontario and St. Timothee, where young Vincenzo watched the thriving bootlegging business outside his window. Nicodemo, trying to support his family, soon got involved in bootlegging and his son followed his example. At an early age, Vincenzo was arrested for a variety of minor offenses. With each arrest, he settled deeper into his criminal career.

Vincenzo and his brothers, Frank and Pep, moved up in the criminal underworld in the years after the Great Depression of

1929. Vincenzo, who now preferred to be called Vic, moved into downtown Montreal to oversee his family's growing nightclub business. From his night haunts, he built a gang that specialized in loan sharking, gambling, extortion, prostitution, and later, food distribution. Throughout the thirties and forties, Cotroni tightened his grip on Montreal, earning the nickname "le Perrain" (the Godfather). In these early years, he used his considerable mediating skills to keep the conflict between rival Italian, French-Canadian, and Anglo gangs at a minimum—and his profit at a maximum.

Frank Cotroni, Vic's brother, returns to Canada in 1979 after serving time in a U.S. federal prison for narcotics violations.

Joe "Bananas" Bonanno, a major player in the U.S Mafia, kept his eye on the up-and-coming Cotroni and, in 1953, decided the time was right for a little foreign investment. Bonanno sent Carmine Galante, his driver and close associate, to pay a visit to the frail, 135-pound Godfather of Montreal. Vic "The Egg"—who was not fond of the moniker, which called attention to his bald head—met Galante at a pizzeria. Perhaps while eating a pizza, Galante made an offer to Cotroni that the Canadian could not refuse. Cotroni had only dabbled in drug running, but Galante suggested that Montreal could become the major hub for the Mafia's lucrative drug trafficking. Since U.S. authorities had clamped down on the New York drug routes, Galante, remebering the good old days of Prohibition, knew that Montreal would be an ideal launching pad for smuggling heroin into the United States. Cotroni accepted the deal but had to accept Galante as boss of the drug-trafficking business.

Galante opened up an electronics store as a front for his drug-smuggling operations. In 1955, a hard-hitting, crime-fighting mayor, Jean Drapeaux, was elected in Montreal. He had Galante deported to the United States because he could not

explain exactly what his occupation was. Bonanno then sent Salvatore Giglio to Montreal, and he ran the operation until 1957, when he too was deported.

Bonanno, tiring of the constant deportation of his henchmen, turned to Cotroni in 1957. Cotroni accepted the position as Bonanno's frontman, greatly increasing his take in the profits, but at the same time accepting the authority of Bonanno. Nevertheless, Cotroni's timing was superb; shortly after he accepted the position, the famous "French Connection" heroin ring was set up. Turkish opium was smuggled to Marseilles, processed into heroin, then shipped to Montreal for delivery into the United States. Cotroni's take from the French Connection was staggering—one of four accounts used to launder money had a balance of $83 million US.

Even though Cotroni had to answer to Bonanno, the profits were worth it. Also, he still had a relatively free hand in his own territory of Montreal. As a demonstration of his firm control and wealth, Cotroni built a magnificent country home that doubled as a convention center for Canadian gangsters. He had a special conference room with chandeliers and a handcrafted walnut boardroom table that could seat two

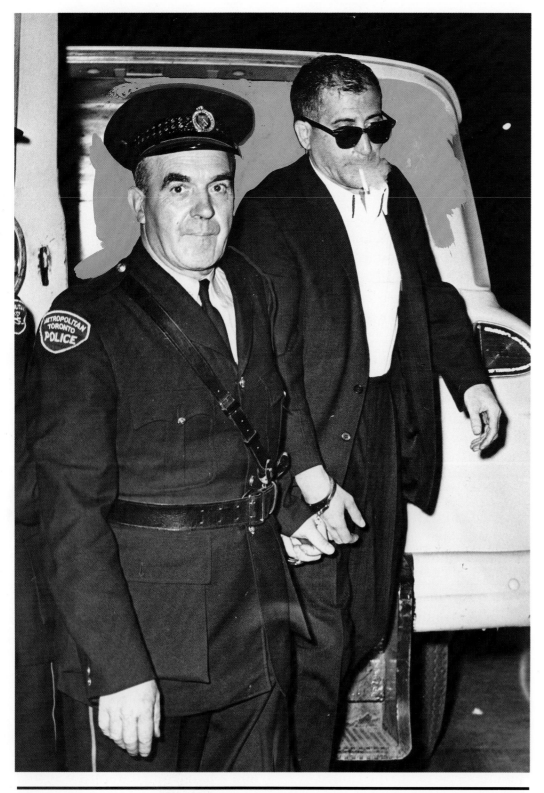

Johnny Papalia, associate of Vic Cotroni and overlord of the Hamilton underworld.

dozen people. The house was built with security and privacy in mind. Careful not to upstage his gangster guests, the diplomatic Cotroni had the master bedroom and guest bedrooms built to the same size and decorated with equal splendor.

The sixties were prosperous years. Cotroni, his brothers, and their close associate, Paolo Viola, worked their magic in Montreal while Johnny "Paps" Papalia managed the Hamilton area. Cotroni scored a major coup when he monopolized the 1967 Expo food contract (unfortunately, there were several cases of food poisoning from the horsemeat that Cotroni tried to pass off as beef). Despite the culinary scandal, the Cotroni family was on top of the Canadian crime scene.

From the height of his power, Cotroni saw some of his closest friends end up behind bars. In the early sixties, his brother Pep was convicted of narcotics smuggling when he unwittingly took on an FBI agent as a courier. Carmine Galante, Cotroni's old friend from the Bonanno family, was sentenced to twelve years for drug-related charges in 1962. Then Joe Bonanno himself went into hiding after his plan to overthrow the other New York families was discovered by the Commission. Cotroni was a lonely man in

Montreal and, more importantly, his future was uncertain as long as Bonanno's life was in danger.

Although Bonanno eventually made tenuous peace with the other New York families in the late sixties, Cotroni's career took a turn for the worse. While Cotroni was busy grooming Paolo Viola as his successor, Canadian authorities were also busy with an undercover investigation of Viola, who had unwittingly rented out an apartment above his pizzeria to an undercover detective known only as Menard. Menard had the nerve to haggle with Viola over the

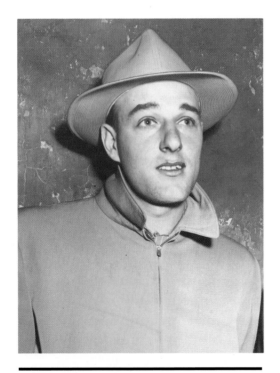

Paul Volpe, seen here in his early years, earned a reputation for brutal violence in the Toronto area.

rent, impressing the Italian; he took a liking to the quiet detective and they became aquaintances. Detective Menard, capitalizing on Viola's friendliness, planted surveillance equipment in the latter's office, eventually collecting enough taped evidence to put Viola in jail. When the arrest was finally made, Viola found out Menard was responsible. While Viola's underlings wanted to kill Menard, Viola emphatically overruled them, saying, "He's a stand-up guy. He's a better f- - - ing soldier than the rest of you!"

Menard had done an excellent job. The tapes also implicated Godfather Vic Cotroni himself, sending him to jail for six months on a minor offense. As he brooded in jail, Cotroni became increasingly angry with his disappointing protégé Viola. When Viola was finally released, he made matters worse by talking far too much about Cotroni's business arrangements. Cotroni was increasingly upset and nervous—his patience for Viola finally ran out. One night Viola was playing cards when a shotgun was placed against his head and fired.

Not long after Paolo's funeral (which had a procession of thirty-one Cadillacs carrying an enormous cargo of flowers), Cotroni received the bad news that his old friend Carmine Galante had been

gunned down in a Brooklyn restaurant. Next, Cotroni's brother Frank was convicted on drug charges and given a five-to-fifteen-year term. Vic Cotroni was hopelessly alone just when he needed help to hold onto his crumbling empire.

When the eighties arrived, contending gang leaders challenged Cotroni's hold on Montreal. In a last-ditch effort to recapture the glory days, Cotroni uncharacteristically turned to violence to move in on the Toronto-Hamilton area. With his Hamilton friend Johnny "Paps" Papalia, he set his sights on Toronto. On November 14, 1983, Paul Volpe, the head of the Toronto underworld, was found shot to death in the trunk of his car at the Pearson International Airport. Rumor had it that Cotroni was behind the hit, but he was unable to capitalize on the temporary power vacuum in Toronto. Cotroni's Machiavellian plan had failed. Vic Cotroni, who had lost his skill as a mediator and proved a failure at using brute force, died in 1984 while his empire was falling to pieces.

After Vic Cotroni's death, Frank Cotroni tried to reestablish his family in the Montreal area but met with limited success. During the late eighties, Iranian and Chinese gangs pushed the Cotroni family into obscurity.

CHAPTER FOUR

DOWN UNDER

We have a war, 24 hours a day, seven days a week, in our cities, towns and countryside. It is a war carried out by criminals who deliberately eroded our rights. They rob, steal and assault, degrade our children with heroin and cocaine, disrupt our economy with massive white collar crime, and have no compunction at living and working outside the law. This is the war we should be fighting now, with the full resources and backing of our government and people.

—Major General Ron Grey, Commissioner of the Australian Federal Police

Whereas it galvanized the North American underworld, Prohibition caused hardly more than a ripple in the relatively calm life of Australian gangsters. The tidal wave of organized crime was not to begin until transoceanic shipping made Australia a hub for the transportation of certain illegal commodities. During the 1960s, New South Wales, the most industrialized and populous of the six Australian states, watched as the small-time crime racket run by the Calabrian "Honoured Society" was overrun by an international, multimillion-dollar crime network largely under the control of an Australian–United States mafiosi partnership. Relatively unknown Australian bosses of both Italian

and Anglo descent were visited by certain U.S. Mafia figures, launching Australian gangsters on new and lucrative enterprises.

As a result of this new partnership, Australian gangsters Bob Trimbole, Lennie "Mr. Big" McPherson, Stan "The Man" Smith, and many others started making fortunes from international drug trafficking, gambling, extortion, and money laundering. But in addition to these typical rackets, Australian gangsters also ventured into previously uncharted territory. The gangsters from down under applied the same racketeering tactics to such unusual criminal enterprises as rare-animal smuggling, shoplifting, and embezzling.

THE DRUG CONNECTION

The sixties were watershed years for the Australian underworld. A sudden flurry of meetings between Chicago gangster Joe Testa and various Australian gangsters signaled the beginning of a business partnership between the American Mafia and the Australian underworld. In 1965, Testa visited Sydney, befriending several Australian criminal figures. Three years later, Australians George Freeman and Stan "The Man" Smith went to see Testa in Chicago, where they were lavishly entertained and then whisked off to Las Vegas for an all-expenses-paid extravaganza. In 1969, Testa returned to Sydney where Freeman, Smith, and Lennie "Mr. Big" McPherson threw a party for him at the Fisherman's Lodge Restaurant at Watsons Bay. The party's finale came when a cake was presented to Testa with the words "Welcome Joe" written across the top. Not long after this party, "Mr. Big" himself traveled to Chicago for a visit with Testa.

Joe Testa was working for Jimmy Fratianno, a powerful New York boss. Although Testa had done a marvelous job of building good working relations with the Australians by 1971, the Austra-

Stan "The Man" Smith, responding to public outrage at his alleged involvement in organized crime, called a press conference and denied taking part in any criminal enterprises.

From left to right: George Freeman, Darcy Dugan, and Lennie McPherson. Freeman believed in forging strong relations with the U.S. Mafia, focusing on drug trafficking.

lians were slow to give up their independence. To help persuade the Australians, Testa delivered a suitcase containing $1 million US in cash to "Mr. Big" McPherson—a gift from Fratianno intended to grease the wheels of a drug-trafficking enterprise that had been moving slowly since 1968. This drug enterprise was the heart

and soul of the United States–Australian partnership. In 1967, Fratianno had sent George "Duke" Countis to take up permanent residence in Australia to serve as his emissary and manager. Countis quickly went to work and contacted the Australian drug smuggler Murray Riley. Soon after their initial contact, a deal

was negotiated with the heroin suppliers of the so-called Golden Triangle, a region comprising parts of Thailand, Laos, and Burma that is to this day the largest producer of opium poppy in the world.

After tapping this rich heroin source, Countis and Riley set up an extensive smuggling system from Thailand to New South Wales. The smugglers relied on maritime routes, secret airstrips, and, occasionally, couriers. All was set to go, but the Australian bosses were slow to tap the new drug supply from the Golden Triangle—until Fratianno's generous gift finally accelerated the pace of heroin smuggling into Australia.

The flood of heroin from the Golden Triangle in the seventies made many gangsters rich, but it also resulted in death and poverty for many Australians. There are twenty thousand heroin addicts in Australia; some die, and many turn to crime to support their habits. Even so, the Australian heroin-using population consumes only one percent of the Golden Triangle's worldwide output.

Heroin is not the only drug used in Australia. An estimated half million citizens smoke marijuana at least once a month. Most of the marijuana is grown in Australia, especially by the Calabrian immigrants who live in Griffith. Bob Trimbole, one of the most colorful of the Griffith growers, made so much money that he devised a scam for laundering his illegally earned income. He fixed horse races by bribing jockeys, doping up horses, and manipulating outrageous odds so he knew exactly which horse

would win and at what odds. By placing well-timed bets, Trimbole could account for his drug money as gambling winnings.

The Griffith growers produce tons of marijuana a year. With the earnings from these lucrative crops, the growers have built splendid houses, which are referred to as "grass castles."

Between heroin and marijuana, drugs account for most of the Australian gangsters' income. However, several uniquely Australian rackets also bring in a hefty profit for the gangsters down under.

Murray Riley eventually ended up in prison for his exploits as a drug smuggler. Ironically, Riley was a policeman before he turned to crime.

WILDLIFE SMUGGLING

It was only a matter of time before wildlife smuggling became big business in Australia. When the drug-smuggling ships and planes arrived at their secret drop-off points, they originally went back to Thailand with empty cargo holds. But by the mid-seventies, Australian gangsters were filling the cargo holds with such exotic animals as galahs, sulphur-crested cockatoos, parrots, koalas, kangaroos, and snakes. Smuggling the unusual wildlife of Australia to Asia and the United States quickly became part of the Australian crime scene. The wildlife smuggling continues to this day—drugs are smuggled in and wildlife is smuggled out. The wildlife smuggling is handled with the same efficiency as heroin smuggling; oftentimes the wildlife is simply traded for the heroin so cash does not have to pass hands twice.

The galah, which is little more than a pest, sulphur-crested cockatoos, and rare parrots cost next to nothing to obtain in Australia; some of them can even be captured in the wild at no cost whatsoever. These rare animals are smuggled into Asian countries and the United States, where they are worth a small fortune. Vinnie smugglers. United States officials cracked one Australian smuggling ring called the "Swiss Connection" when 150 snakes, lizards, and crocodiles were intercepted while en route to Switzerland from Queensland. The final destination of the shipment was Philadelphia, the American center for illegal rare-animal importation. Despite the demise of Testa and the "Swiss Connection," Australian wildlife is still smuggled out of the country.

KANGAROO GANGS

Shoplifting, usually thought of as the province of thieving employees, rebel teenagers, and kleptomaniacs, is also a highly sophisticated, internationally organized crime operation based in Sydney. Arthur "The Duke" Delaney is the suspected mastermind of a professional shoplifting syndicate that pillages Australian

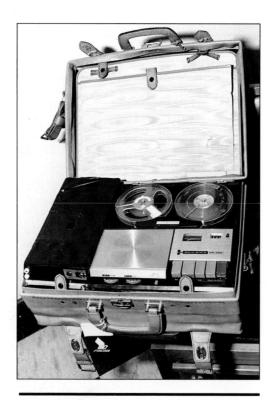

Individual couriers often used secret compartments in personal luggage to smuggle valuable birds out of Australia. At first glance, this briefcase appears to house a tape recorder.

Teresa, the biggest American client of the bird-smuggling operation, put out a mere $3,000 US for a load of birds that would have been worth $2 million US in the United States if the birds had not been seized by authorities.

In 1984, Teresa, facing charges of conspiring to smuggle rare birds into the United States, agreed to give information about the wildlife smuggling rather than go to jail. Teresa's information proved helpful in nabbing other smugglers—and not just bird

As the tape recorder is disassembled by removing the battery cover and left reel, a secret compartment is revealed. Hidden in the compartment are four special containers used to protect the valuable birds.

Vinnie Teresa, Australia's most valuable customer in the United States, attracted the attention of U.S. and Australian customs officials and was eventually arrested.

and major European cities. This Australian shoplifting syndicate has no equal in the world.

The damage done by these professional shoplifting gangs in London is so profound that Scotland Yard has a special task force to track down and arrest the so-called Kangaroo Gangs.

The Australian shoplifters are trained at a school run by Delaney, where they learn the basic strategies of effective shoplifting. One popular scam is for a man and woman to pose as a recently engaged couple discussing which wedding ring to buy. Waiting for the right moment, the pair then dashes off with the whole tray of rings. Another ploy is to steal a number of dresses and then send in a series of gang members the next day who pose as unsatisfied customers demanding a cash refund.

Shoplifting is not considered a serious crime in most countries so the Kangaroo Gangs will undoubtedly continue their exploits. The fines that shoplifters receive amount to little more than a slap on the wrist when compared to the profits, which are enormous.

THE KNIGHTS OF MALTA

Although not a gangster in the classic sense, Ivan Markovic traveled among the gangster elite of Australia and the United States. Markovic, an immigrant from Eastern Europe, was an Australian con artist who devised an ingenious scam that made him millions. Markovic set up an office for the Knights of Malta at the United Nations headquarters in New York. The legitimate Knights of Malta organization has a long history of defending Christianity that dates all the way back to the Crusades, and today is a papal order that is respected the world over. Markovic, using the reputation of the real Knights of Malta and his respectable United Nations address, approached wealthy Australians and asked for donations to his own bogus philanthropic organization.

He so eloquently explained the many noble projects that he and his fellow knights were already involved in, that many of his vic-

Rudy Tham, a member of the San Francisco Teamsters Union, was one of Ivan Markovic's first U.S. initiates in the Knights of Malta. Tham had close ties with the Mafia and had been indicted for conspiracy and extortion.

tims donated thousands of dollars in return for induction into the Knights of Malta as full knights. Needless to say, the whole operation was a scam; Markovic's Knights of Malta was an unlicensed takeoff of the real papal order and Markovic kept all the contributions for his own profit.

Markovic's early takers included businessmen and lawyers who were happy to donate large sums of money in return for the special privileges that accompany knighthood: diplomatic passports, diplomatic immunity, fancy knight regalia, and the prestige of belonging to a papal order. Also, the pomp and circumstance surrounding the whole induction ceremony and annual meetings was very seductive.

On one occasion, twenty-three soon-to-be-knights flew all the way to Rome, where they stayed at the posh Hotel Excelsior. The following day the somber knighting ceremony was led by a Cardinal at what was called the Basilica di St. Nicola (actually an abandoned casino trumped up for the occasion). The twenty-three donors were knighted, and their wallets lightened.

Markovic's scam was working wonderfully until several unlikely candidates were knighted. First, Perce Galae, the undisputed head of the illegal casino called the Forbes Club, was knighted. Then Bela Csidei, a marijuana grower, tried to avoid arrest by using a passport issued by the Knights of Malta to claim diplomatic immunity. These incidents began to catch the public's attention, bringing Ivan Markovic under close scrutiny.

Although "Sir Bela" could not produce the passport and was eventually put in jail, he had provided Markovic with a bridge to the United States. Bela was close with Rudy Tham, the San Francisco leader of the Teamsters Union. Markovic worked his magic on Tham, who went so far as to appropriate union funds to have himself knighted. Markovic also asked Tham to spread the word to other wealthy individuals who might be interested in contributing to charity.

Predictably enough, the only wealthy people that Tham knew were high-level gangsters. Accordingly, Tham contacted Jimmy Fratianno, who quickly realized that Markovic was a con man and that the Knights of Malta was a sham. Tham told Fratianno, "This is a very exclusive order...in fact, I just got in myself," to which Fratianno sharply replied, "Bullshit, not if you're in it, buddy...sounds like a high-class scam."

Fratianno, rather than blow the whistle on Markovic, asked Markovic to help him with some Mafia business. Fratianno, always looking to make money, wanted to get Frank Sinatra to sing at a few New York locations and control the ticket sales. Fratianno suggested that Markovic could have Sinatra knighted in exchange for singing at benefits for the order. Although the plan failed, the whole episode has haunted Sinatra to this day.

Markovic continued to travel the world with his beauty-queen daughter, Eve. A dashing figure in his knight regalia, Markovic persuaded countless individuals to donate money to his cause. Quite often, he worked with Fratianno to induct individuals from whom Fratianno wanted favors. The donors, so excited about becoming knights, never asked to see where their donations went. Markovic lived more like a king than a knight until his operation was exposed in 1985. His New York United Nations office was closed and Markovic fled to West Germany, where he avoided prosecution for fraud.

Frank Sinatra, seen here dining with other Hollywood stars, never fell for Markovic's confidence game; he refused to become a member of the Knights of Malta.

CHAPTER FIVE

BRITAIN

Reginald Kray and his girlfriend Frances Shea, 1965.

When it comes to great gangsters and organized crime, Britain cannot compete with the three nations she produced. A trip through the famous Madame Tussaud's Wax Museum in London reveals that the truly legendary British criminals are known for their mysterious, blood-curdling murders—Jack the Ripper being the most famous of them all. Gangsters rarely receive much attention in Britain, primarily because gang activities tend to occur on a local level and are fairly disorganized.

There are many reasons why criminal organizations such as the Mafia have never become a major national problem in Britain, but two explanations seem most plausible. Some suggest that since gambling and the use of some drugs are legal in Britain, the government has effectively removed the need for organized crime. Another sound argument suggests that the absence of a large southern Italian population in the early 1900s prevented the introduction of the highly organized principles of the Mafia. Whatever the case, the Mafia is not a powerful force in Britain to this day.

This is not to say that gangs do not exist in Britain. Gangsters occasionally become a serious threat to the government. Two notable gangsters (although they cannot be found in Tussaud's house of wax) are the twin brothers Reginald and Ronald Kray. During the 1960s, the twins started what they called "The Firm," the most notorious gangster outfit in British history. Specializing in brutal protection rackets and extortion, the Krays terrorized the East End of London and had visions of taking over the entire city. The story of the rise and fall of the Kray "Firm" is a truly macabre tale that encapsulates the best and the worst of British gang lore.

On October 24, 1933, Violet Kray gave birth to almost completely identical twin boys. Reginald was the older, genetically dominant brother and Ronald was the younger twin, who possessed a mole below his collarbone—the only way to tell the two apart.

The East End of London was a dirty, tough, and dangerous place to grow up, but Violet Kray always looked out for her twins. It became even more dangerous when World War II broke out and London came under German aerial attack. The twins fled the East End for the safety of the country, but only for a short while; like a strong magnet, the Cockney neighborhood drew the young twins back. The Daniel Street School was open only sporadically during the war and Reggie and Ronnie attended only if they felt in the mood. Even when they did decide to attend classes, the twins were far more interested in fighting than studying. They picked fights on the playground and, foretelling the future, fought side by side. They were an unbeatable team.

Soon the young toughs tired of the playground pickings and graduated to the streets of the East End. Waiting on a corner,

The Kray brothers: Reginald (left), his twin brother, Ronald (right), and Charles (center) shake hands after being convicted of murder and accessory to murder.

they would randomly attack pedestrians and sometimes rob their victims. Arresting Reggie or Ronnie was extremely problematic because witnesses could not tell the police which one was responsible. The Krays quickly realized they had a built-in defense against arrest.

Their juvenile delinquency worsened in the mid-forties until a wise probation officer tried to channel their energy into a more productive, or at least legal, pas-

time—boxing. The boys joined the Mansford Amateur Boxing Club and proved to be outstanding boxers. Building muscles by hoisting heavy loads of fish at the London Fish Market by day, the twins were tearing up the canvas at night. They had found an outlet for their violent tendencies—at least for a short while.

After turning professional, their boxing careers took a turn for the worse. Along with their older brother, Charles, they were unable to distinguish themselves in the pro ranks and began drifting into anonymity.

Their pro career was cut short when they were called up for National Service in 1950. The Krays reported to the Royal Fusiliers recruiting station at the Tower of London, where they proceeded to punch out the sergeant in charge and flee back to their East End haunts. The brothers were not good at keeping a low profile and were soon caught and returned, in handcuffs, to military service. Once again, the Krays overpowered the guards and raced back to the East End in a last-ditch effort to avoid the confines of a military life. Only twenty-four hours later, the brothers were facing a court-martial and were sentenced to nine months at Shepton Mallet, a military prison in the West Country.

The Krays flouted military authority while at Shepton, stripping one officer of his red sash of office and then dumping their slops over the "demoted" gentleman. The military was happy to finally be rid of the crazy brothers after nine months. The Krays soon became a problem for the civilian authorities.

Upon leaving the National Service, Reggie and Ronnie went into the employ of Jack "Spot" (so called because he always

Ronald Kray, who never lost touch with the boxing world, chatting with former world heavyweight champion Joe Louis.

seemed to be on the spot at any crime). Spot, a contending underworld boss, was the landlord and protector for the bookmaking agencies and he used the twins as rent collectors. With their excellent boxing skills, they displayed a knack for making bookmakers pay up.

The Krays soon left Spot's operation because he was losing an underworld fight with Billy Hill, a rival gang leader. Thinking their

fortunes were brighter as self-employed thugs, they opened up a billiards hall as the headquarters for their operations.

The novices were soon approached by a group of Maltese who wanted to speak to the Krays about protection; in other words, if the Krays did not pay a fixed amount to the Maltese then something disastrous would happen to the twins or their billiards hall. Ronald cut the conversation short, so to speak, by rushing the waiting car and driving a bayonet through its roof, frightening the Maltese away.

Ronald, who had emerged as the more dominant of the brothers even though he was younger, fancied himself quite a fighter with the bayonet. Both twins learned how to fight with a variety of antiquated weapons like swords and daggers. On one occasion, Ronnie stabbed a man outside the Britannia pub in full view of many witnesses. He was arrested for causing grievous bodily harm and, even though Reggie tried to confuse the witnesses by showing up in court, was sentenced to three years in prison. Once at Winchester Prison, Ronnie was declared criminally insane and transferred to Long Grove Mental Hospital. There is reason to believe Ronnie feigned madness to escape the harsh surroundings of prison for the more amenable view at Long Grove. The plan worked but with one snag: Ronnie's three-year sentence was now an indefinite term of incarceration until the doctors decided he was cured. He and his brother devised an ingenious escape plan.

On a Monday in 1958, Reggie—decked out in a navy blue suit, gray checked shirt, and black shoes—and three friends came to visit Ronnie. Coincidentally, Ronnie had dressed up for the visit in a navy blue suit, gray checked shirt, and black shoes. The brothers chatted and then one of them asked the guard if he could get some tea. Thinking it was Reggie, the guard let the twin out of the cell. Rather than getting tea, Ronnie kept walking right out of the hospital to freedom. When the three friends and Reggie got up to leave, the guard tried to stop Reggie from leaving, thinking he was Ronnie. Reggie explained that they had no grounds to hold him since he was just a visitor. To

Billy Hill, the underworld boss of the East End before the Kray twins seized power.

prove his point he reminded the guard and doctors that Ronnie had a mole below his collarbone, which he did not have. The Kray brothers had pulled the old switcheroo.

Ronnie had escaped to prove his ability to function in the outside world, thus earning a re-examination by the doctors that would end his stay at Long Grove. He was declared sane but, in view of his escape, was required to serve a short sentence at Winchester Prison.

Not long after both brothers were back on the streets, Reggie was arrested for extortion and sentenced to eighteen months. After Reggie's release, the twins, with the help of their older, more respectable brother, Charles, made a go at honest business. In 1960, the three brothers opened up the Double R club (they borrowed the Rolls Royce emblem). They made a point of following liquor license rules and put on the trappings of a legitimate business. But it was only a matter of time before the twins started regressing to their old ways.

While managing the Double R, the twins came up with an idea that would eventually earn them fame. "The Firm," as they called it, was originally intended to be a wholly legal business, but it was soon corrupted into an organiza-

Reginald Kray and Frances Shea finally wed on April 20, 1965. Ronald Kray was a homosexual and never married.

tion devoted to extortion, protection, forgery, drug running, and gambling.

The Firm got its start when the brothers opened an illegal gambling house on the top floor of their club. To shut down the Double R's competition, they beat up the managers of other clubs. However, the authorities took note of the Kray's illegal practices and raided the Double R, eventually shutting it down.

Without a club of their own, the Krays tried to open up a series of new clubs, all of them ending in failure. The brothers sought notoriety and respect among high society, so they targeted the posh clubs in the West End of London. To the brothers' dismay, however, wherever they went, their reputations soon followed, and none of the West Enders would frequent their clubs.

The Firm took a new tack and began muscling in on existing West End clubs for a cut of the action. In 1965, the Krays were charged with threatening a club manager with bodily harm unless he turned over 50 percent of his earnings to The Firm. The twins were acquitted and continued to threaten other managers, most of whom were too afraid to go the police.

The duo's image was much improved with the opening of the

George Cornell, friend of the imprisoned John Richardson, brazenly vowed to continue the attack on the Krays' control of the East End even though the Richardson gang was virtually disbanded.

high-class El Morocco club and Reggie's marriage to the young Frances Shea. The respect and publicity that they so badly craved was finally coming their way. However, as with any great tragedy, their apparent success was actually the beginning of their fall.

Reggie's marriage fell apart when the seventeen-year-old Frances claimed that Reggie physically and psychologically abused her and demanded a divorce. A long, bitter separation followed, but Frances had already fallen into a serious depression before

the divorce became final. She eventually killed herself with a barbiturate overdose.

The public sensation surrounding Frances Shea's death greatly damaged Reggie's reputation. Perhaps more significantly, the brothers' efforts to gain respect were thwarted by an outbreak of gang violence on the East End. An upstart gang led by John Richardson attempted to muscle in on the Krays' East End business, leading to a shootout at a local pub. Richardson hoped to gain control of the East End by killing off certain Kray enforcers, but the plan backfired and Richardson found himself behind bars instead.

The Richardson trial was a public sensation. The testimony described unspeakable tortures, blackmail, and grand designs of launching a citywide gang. Richardson and his men were convicted and put away for long sentences. Indirectly, the Krays were implicated in the trial and Scotland Yard set their sights on the twins.

The Krays, unaware that Scotland Yard was closing in, actually breathed easier now that Richardson and his gang were locked away. But they still feared that George Cornell, a top Richardson aide who had avoided arrest, was planning to continue his boss'

The Blind Beggar Pub after the murder of George Cornell. The mark on the chair leg nearest the cash register is believed to have been caused by a bullet from Ronald Kray's gun.

fectly identical lives. The psychological bond between the twin brothers was demented and powerful; Ronnie had killed and now expected his brother to do the same. Their target was Jack "The Hat" McVitie.

McVitie, who got his nickname because he always wore a hat to cover his balding head, had been slow in performing a job for the Krays so they decided to teach him a lesson. The twins invited him to a party. McVitie did not know that he was the guest of honor and main attraction for the evening. While McVitie thought he

attempts at conquest. Also, Cornell publicly ridiculed Ronnie for his homosexual affairs. The Krays decided to eliminate Cornell, thinking this would solidify their claim on the East End and allow them to expand to other London areas.

The hit was quick and efficient. Cornell was drinking at the Blind Beggar, a pub in the Krays' territory, when Ronald waltzed in without saying a word and fired a nine-millimeter bullet right between Cornell's eyes. Even though there were many witnesses, they all claimed to have seen nothing—a fitting explanation for patrons of the Blind Beggar.

The execution-style murder of Cornell intensified the public's outrage, which had already built to a frenzy after the Richardson trial. Scotland Yard moved into action, but were unable to cure the "temporary blindness" of the frightened witnesses. The detectives believed that once the Krays were arrested for lesser crimes the witnesses to the murder would no longer be afraid to give testimony.

The twins made matters worse when they killed again. It is often said that the bond between identical twins is so strong that even when separated at birth the twins will end up leading remarkably similar lives. Ronnie and Reggie, hardly ever apart, tried to live per-

In a rare moment, Jack "The Hat" McVitie without his hat. McVitie was a bumbling petty criminal who was the brunt of many jokes in the East End.

was going to just another party, the Krays' other guests knew that they were attending McVitie's premeditated murder.

When McVitie opened the door, he was greeted by Reggie, who pointed a pistol at McVitie's bald head and pulled the trigger. The firing mechanism failed, so Reggie pulled the trigger again, but still the gun would not fire. In a panic, McVitie rushed for the window and tried to jump through the glass, but Ronnie and the other guests wrestled him to the ground. Reggie, encouraged by Ronnie, ran into the kitchen and came back with a twelve-inch (30cm) carving knife and plunged the knife into McVitie's face. Reggie stabbed him in virtually every part of his body until Jack The Hat was dead in a pool of his own blood.

When the body was found by detectives, they once again could not find any witnesses to the murder. By this time, Scotland Yard was sure that there were plenty of witnesses to both the Cornell and McVitie murders who were just too afraid to come forward while the Krays were walking the streets. The detectives decided to build a strong case against the twins for forgery, drug dealing, and extortion in hopes that their arrest would prompt witnesses to the two murders to come forward.

Scotland Yard watched the Kray twins with increasing diligence after the murder of George Cornell.

Scotland Yard took action on May 8, 1968, in a well-coordinated raid that toppled the Firm. Ronald was arrested while in bed with a young boy and Reggie was discovered with a young woman. Only hours after the twins were behind bars, the telephones were ringing off the hook at Scotland Yard. Just as the detectives had hoped, the witnesses to the Cornell and McVitie murders had suddenly regained their memories.

Ronnie and Reggie were both found guilty on a variety of charges: the sentences amounted to life in prison. Amazingly, the twins proclaimed their innocence until the very end. The brothers remain in jail today.

CONCLUSION

The history of gangsterism is inextricably connected to the history of the Mafia. There were gangsters before the Mafia and there will be gangsters if ever the Mafia is to disappear, but the Mafia at the height of its power shaped the very nature of organized crime. For that reason, the Mafia deserves a special place in the history of organized crime.

Today the Mafia's hold on international organized crime has been broken by vigorous competition from other gangs the world over. However, no one crime syndicate is likely to have the same power that the Mafia enjoyed in the fifties. Thanks to the wealth of films and books about the golden age of the Mafia, no one is likely to forget how simple gang activities were transformed into an international empire.

PHOTO CREDITS

© Archive Photos: p. 26

© Canada Wide Feature Services Ltd.: pp. 41 top, 42, 43, 44, 45

© City of Toronto Archives: p. 41 bottom right

© John Fairfax Group Pty Ltd. Feature Bureau: p. 47

© FPG International: pp. 7 top, 15, 20, 23, 25, 29, 31

© LDE/Archive Photos: pp. 54, 55, 56, 57, 58

© Rice/John Fairfax Group Pty Ltd. Feature Bureau: p. 50

© Ross/John Fairfax Group Pty Ltd. Feature Bureau: p. 49

© Joseph Sherman/FPG International: p. 10

© Syndication International: pp. 59, 60

© Wide World Photos: pp. 6, 7 bottom right, 8, 9, 11, 13, 16, 19, 22, 24, 28, 33, 34, 35, 36, 37, 38, 39, 40, 51, 52, 53, 61

© Wright/John Fairfax Group Pty Ltd. Feature Bureau: p. 48

FURTHER READING

Albini, Joseph L. *The American Mafia: Genesis of a Legend*. New York: Appleton-Century-Crofts, 1971.

Balsamo, William, and George Carpozi, Jr. *Under The Clock*. Far Hills, N. J.: New Horizon Press, 1988.

Bottom, Bob. *Connections: Crime, Rackets, and Networks of Influence Down-Under*. South Melbourne: Sun Books, 1985.

Bottom, Bob. *Connections II: Crime, Rackets, and Networks of Influence in Australia*. South Melbourne: Sun Books, 1987.

Campbell, Rodney. *The Luciano Project: The Secret Wartime Collaboration of the Mafia and the U.S. Navy*. New York: McGraw-Hill, 1977.

Cummings, John. *Goombatta: The Improbable Rise and Fall of John Gotti and His Gang*. Boston: Little, Brown, 1990.

Davis, John H. *Mafia Kingfish: Carlos Marcello and the Assassination of John F. Kennedy*. New York: McGraw-Hill, 1989.

Dubro, James. *Mob Rule: Inside the Canadian Mafia*. Toronto: Macmillan of Canada, 1985.

Edwards, Peter. *Blood Brothers: How Canada's Most Powerful Mafia Family Runs its Business*. Toronto: Key Porter Books, 1990.

Eisenberg, Dennis. *Meyer Lansky: Mogul of the Mob*. New York: Paddington Press (distributed by Grosset & Dunlap), 1979.

Fox, Stephen R. *Blood and Power: Organized Crime in Twentieth-Century America*. New York: William Morrow, 1989.

Kobler, John. *Capone: The Life and World of Al Capone*. New York: Putnam, 1971.

McFadden, Robert. "Meyer Lansky is Dead at 81; Financial Wizard of Organized Crime," *The New York Times*. January 16, 1983.

Nash, Jay Robert. *Encyclopedia of World Crime: Criminal Justice, Criminology, and Law Enforcement*. Wilmette, Ill.: CrimeBooks, 1989–1990.

Pearson, John. *The Profession of Violence: The Rise and Fall of the Kray Twins*. New York: Saturday Review Press, 1972.

Pileggi, Nicholas. *Wiseguy: Life in a Mafia Family*. New York: Simon & Schuster, 1985.

Puzo, Mario. *The Godfather*. New York: Putnam, 1969.

Reuter, Peter. *Disorganized Crime: The Economics of the Visible Hand*. Cambridge, Mass.: MIT Press, 1983.

Sifakis, Carl. *The Mafia Encyclopedia*. New York: Facts on File, 1987.

Taylor, Laurie. *The Underworld*. Oxford, England: Blackwell, 1984.

FILMS

Bugsy (1991). Directed by Barry Levinson.

Force of Evil (1948). Directed by Abraham Polonsky.

The Godfather (1972). Directed by Francis Ford Coppola.

The Godfather II (1974). Directed by Francis Ford Coppola.

The Godfather III (1991). Directed by Francis Ford Coppola.

Goodfellas (1990). Directed by Martin Scorsese.

The Grifters (1990). Directed by Stephen Frears.

Key Largo (1948). Directed by John Huston.

The Krays (1990). Directed by Peter Mebak.

Little Caesar (1930). Directed by Marvyn LeRoy.

Miller's Crossing (1990). Directed by Joel Coen.

New Jack City (1991). Directed by Mario Van Peebles.

Once Upon a Time In America (1984). Directed by Sergio Leone.

Petrified Forest (1936). Directed by Archie Mayo.

Public Enemy (1931). Directed by William Wellman.

Roaring Twenties (1939). Directed by Raoul Walsh.

Scarface (1932). Directed by Howard Hawks.

Scarface (1983). Directed by Brian DePalma.

The Untouchables (1987). Directed by Brian DePalma.

The Untouchables: The Scarface Mob (1959). Directed by Phil Karlson.

White Heat (1949). Directed by Raoul Walsh.

INDEX